Anis Zaman

Statistical and Semantic Similarity between English Sentences

Anis Zaman

Statistical and Semantic Similarity between English Sentences

LAP LAMBERT Academic Publishing

Impressum / Imprint

Bibliografische Information der Deutschen Nationalbibliothek: Die Deutsche Nationalbibliothek verzeichnet diese Publikation in der Deutschen Nationalbibliografie; detaillierte bibliografische Daten sind im Internet über http://dnb.d-nb.de abrufbar.

Alle in diesem Buch genannten Marken und Produktnamen unterliegen warenzeichen-, marken- oder patentrechtlichem Schutz bzw. sind Warenzeichen oder eingetragene Warenzeichen der jeweiligen Inhaber. Die Wiedergabe von Marken, Produktnamen, Gebrauchsnamen, Handelsnamen, Warenbezeichnungen u.s.w. in diesem Werk berechtigt auch ohne besondere Kennzeichnung nicht zu der Annahme, dass solche Namen im Sinne der Warenzeichen- und Markenschutzgesetzgebung als frei zu betrachten wären und daher von jedermann benutzt werden dürften.

Bibliographic information published by the Deutsche Nationalbibliothek: The Deutsche Nationalbibliothek lists this publication in the Deutsche Nationalbibliografie; detailed bibliographic data are available in the Internet at http://dnb.d-nb.de.

Any brand names and product names mentioned in this book are subject to trademark, brand or patent protection and are trademarks or registered trademarks of their respective holders. The use of brand names, product names, common names, trade names, product descriptions etc. even without a particular marking in this works is in no way to be construed to mean that such names may be regarded as unrestricted in respect of trademark and brand protection legislation and could thus be used by anyone.

Coverbild / Cover image: www.ingimage.com

Verlag / Publisher:
LAP LAMBERT Academic Publishing
ist ein Imprint der / is a trademark of
OmniScriptum GmbH & Co. KG
Heinrich-Böcking-Str. 6-8, 66121 Saarbrücken, Deutschland / Germany
Email: info@lap-publishing.com

Herstellung: siehe letzte Seite /
Printed at: see last page
ISBN: 978-3-659-61638-9

Zugl. / Approved by: New York, Bard College, 12504

Abstract

English sentence similarity measure is used in a vast number of applications such as online web page information retrieval systems, online advertisements, question answering dialogue systems, text summarization, text mining. Over the years, a number of algorithms have been proposed for this difficult problem, but none of the proposed algorithms give sufficient good answer.

In this project, we explore three different algorithms for computing English sentence similarity. The first algorithm, which is well-explored in the literature [Salton and Buckley, 1988, Wu and Salton, 1981], weights words in each sentence according to term frequency and inverse document frequency (*tf-idf*) and uses no semantic information. The second algorithm uses measures of the semantic distance between words belonging to the same part of speech. The third algorithm combines the *tf-idf* scores and the semantic distance scores between words.

We evaluate the performance of the second and third algorithms on two data sets: O'Shea's set of sentence pairs with human similarity judgements [Li et al., Aug, Rubenstein and Goodenough, 1965], and Microsoft Research's sentence-level paraphrase dataset [Rus et al., 2012]. On O'Shea's data set, the third algorithm more accurately matches human judgments than the second. On the Microsoft data set, there was not a significant difference between the two algorithms.

Contents

Abstract   1

Dedication   6

Acknowledgments   7

1   Introduction   8

2   Background   10
   2.1   Term Frequency and Inverse Document Frequency 10
   2.2   Stanford POS Tagger 12
   2.3   WordNet 13
   2.4   Word Sense Disambiguation using Personalized Page Rank 14
   2.5   What is Semantic distance? 15
   2.6   Wikipedia and Simple Wikipedia 16
   2.7   Semantic Similarity Benchmark Data Sets 17
       2.7.1   Human judged sentence pairs 18
       2.7.2   SEMILAR: The Semantic Similarity Corpus 19
   2.8   Correlation and Covariance 20
   2.9   Related Works 21

3   Paragraph Alignment   22
   3.1   Why use *tf-idf* weighting scheme? 23
   3.2   What is the advantage of aligning paragraphs? 24
   3.3   How are paragraphs aligned? 25

4   Sentence Alignment   30
   4.1   Using term frequency and inverse document frequency *tf-idf* 31
       4.1.1   Overview of the Algorithm 32
       4.1.2   Pure tf-idf: An algorithm for computing sentence similarity using tf-idf . . . 33
   4.2   Using semantic only 36

	4.2.1	Overview of the algorithm	37
	4.2.2	Semantic: An algorithm for computing sentence similarity using only semantic distance	38
4.3	Using both semantic distance and *tf-idf*		41
	4.3.1	Combined: An algorithm for computing sentence similarity using tf-idf and semantic distance scores	42

5 Evaluation **45**

| 5.1 | Using O'Shea's 65 Sentence Pairs: | 46 |
| 5.2 | Microsoft Paraphrase | 48 |

6 Discussion **54**

7 Appendix **57**

References **63**

List of Figures

2.2.1 An example a tagged sentence by Stanford POS Tagger 12
2.3.1 An example of WordNet representation 14
2.4.1 An example of word sense disambiguation problem 15
2.5.1 Example of a semantic distance between concepts 16

3.3.1 Example of a paragraph alignment 27
3.3.2 Flow diagram for paragraph alignment 28

4.1.1 The flow diagram of the tf-idf algorithm 36
4.2.1 Computing sentence similarity using the Semantic algorithm 40
4.2.2 The flow diagram of the Semantic algorithm 40
4.3.1 The flow diagram of the Combined algorithm 44

5.1.1 Scatter plot for **Semantic** algorithm 47
5.1.2 Scatter plot for **Combined** algorithm 48
5.2.1 Similarity score distribution for **Semantic** algorithm on **Original** 51
5.2.2 Similarity score distribution for **Semantic** algorithm on **Shuffled** 52
5.2.3 Similarity score distribution for **Combined** algorithm on **Original** 52
5.2.4 Similarity score distribution for **Combined** algorithm on **Shuffled** 53

List of Algorithms

1   filterWords(P) 25
2   Paragraph alignment algorithm 26
3   computeTfidf(P, Col) 33
4   Sentence alignment using tf-idf 34
5   Sentence alignment algorithm using semantic distance 38
6   Sentence alignment algorithm using semantic distance and *tf-idf* 42

Dedication

To Maa, Baba, Bristy and my uncle Jasim for their constant support, encouragement and unconditional love.

I love you all dearly.

Acknowledgments

My deepest gratitude goes first to my advisor Dr. Rebecca Thomas, who gave me the freedom to explore on my own idea, and at the same time guided me whenever my steps were faltered. Her patience and support helped me overcome many crisis situations and finish this project.

I am also very grateful to Dr. Sven Anderson and Dr.Samuel Hsiao for their many insightful advices and discussions. Whenever I walked into Sven's office, he was always there to listen and guide me. I would like to acknowledge Dr.Samuel Hsiao for helping me understand the statistical part of my thesis.

I would like to thank Nabil, a great friend, who was always willing to help and gave his best suggestions. It would have been a lonely lab without him. Many thanks to Blagoy for being an amazing person with great humor, awesome friend, great colleague, and for helping me in so many things. I cannot list how many times you helped me on different things. I cannot but mention about those late night FIFA with Nabil and Blagoy. Those study breaks were one of the most important factors that kept me going in this project

I am grateful to Prabarna and Will for reading hundreds of sentence pairs for me and for supporting me through many difficult times. I want to thank Kevin for being my Squash buddy, Steven for encouraging me all the time. Finally, I want to thank Lamiya for being a great friend, who supported me, encouraged me and more importantly believed in me. I am grateful to have a friend like you.

During my stay at Bard, I made many amazing friends who always supported me and stood by me and helped me in my difficult times. I am grateful to all those who have given me their friendship, put up with my odd hours, and provided me with lifts and practical help.

Above ground, I am indebted to my mom, dad, sister and my uncle who supported me all the time.

1
Introduction

As of December 30, 2011, 56.6% of the data in the World Wide Web are in English and 27% of Internet users browse the World Wide Web in English[1]. The amount of information in the Internet is increasing at a massive rate of 20 terabytes per month[2]. Majority of the data are in the form of texts. Having such a large amount of data is a great privilege, but at the same time, it is difficult to manage and filter appropriate information. Information Retrieval (IR) systems help people find accurate information and access it. But what if the request from the user is too long or ambiguous and the IR systems fail to return the correct information?

One way the IR systems can manage this large amount of information is by summarizing texts, discarding superfluous details. In order to do automatic summarization/simplification the IR systems need the knowledge to distinguish between simplified and unsimplified texts. Using this knowledge base, various Machine Learning techniques can be used to train the IR systems. But the problem is that there are not many training data. One way to produce such a dataset is to take candidate pairs of simplified/unsimplified texts and check whether they actually are sufficiently

---

[1] http://en.wikipedia.org/wiki/Languages_used_on_the_Internet#Internet_users_by_language
[2] http://archive.org/about/faqs.php#9

semantically similar to serve as good training data. The work presented in this project can help generate good training data to produce simplifiers.

In this thesis, we present three different algorithms for computing semantic similarity between short texts of sentence length. The first algorithm is purely statistical; it uses term frequency and inverse document frequency *(tf-idf)* weighting for computing sentence similarity. This approach treats sentences as vectors and measures sentence similarity by computing cosine similarity between the vectors. The second algorithm uses the semantic distance between important words from two sentences and combines these scores to compute sentence similarity. The last algorithm combines the two previous algorithms by weighting the semantic distance scores with the *tf-idf* weight of the words.

2
Background

2.1 Term Frequency and Inverse Document Frequency

In Natural Language Processing (NLP) research a very common statistical assumption is that words that appear less frequently in a content are considered as more informative than the commonly occurring words. For example, words such as *somehow* and *terminate* may appear many times in a document or in a collection of documents. But most likely, *terminate* is a better keyword than *somehow* because the word *terminate* is less common in general usage. Hence, low frequency words tend to be rich in content. Term frequency and inverse document frequency (*tf-idf*) [Manning et al., 2008] is a strategy coined by Information Retrieval (IR) researchers to capture this idea. The *tf-idf* weighting is a very commonly used technique to extract information about the importance of a term or word in a document in a corpus, or in a collection of documents. The *tf-idf* consists of two parts, namely term frequency, denoted as *tf(t,d)* and inverse document frequency, denoted by $idf(t, D)$ where d is a document in a collection of documents (or a corpus) D and t is a term. Term frequency is a way to assign weight to term in a document based on the number of times the term appears in the document. Inverse document frequency is a measure of how rare or common a particular word or term is in a collection of documents. The following formula computes the $tf(t,d)$, $idf(t,D,)$ and $tf\text{-}idf(t,d,D)$ respectively:

$$tf(t,d) = \frac{frequency(t,d)}{max\{frequency(w,d) : w \in d\}} \qquad (2.1.1)$$

$$idf(t,D) = log\frac{|D|}{|\{d \in D : t \in d\}|} \qquad (2.1.2)$$

$$tf\text{-}idf(t,d,D) = tf(t,d) \times idf(t,D) \qquad (2.1.3)$$

A high term frequency and a low document frequency lead to a high *tf-idf* weight. Thus common terms tend to have low weights because they have low *idf* values. Notice that the ratio in the *idf* formula is always greater than or equal to 1, and the value of the *tf-idf* is greater than or equal to 0. When a word or a term appears in more documents the ratio inside the *idf's* log function approaches 1, bringing the *tf-idf* closer to 0. An example of this process is given below.

In a collection of documents on financial industry, it is likely that the term *finance* will appear in almost every document. Thus *finance* is not a distinguishing word. In order to attenuate the effect of such frequently occurring words in the collection, the idea of rare terms being more informative than the frequent terms comes into play. Also, words such as *high*, *increase*, *line*, *upward*, *backward*, and other general so-called *stop words* appear in lots of documents when describing different contexts. Although these words appear many times, their high frequency is not a great indication of their relevance or richness in content. A way to solve this problem is to assign small positive weight to frequent terms. These weights are much smaller than the weights assigned to rare terms.

In summary, *tf-idf* prevents all terms or words in a document from being considered equally important when it comes to assessing relevancy to a query. In fact, certain terms have little or no discriminating power in determining relevance. In this thesis, one of the algorithms primarily only uses this principle of *tf-idf*.

2.2 Stanford POS Tagger

The Stanford Part-Of-Speech Tagger (POS Tagger) [Klein and Manning, 2003] is a software that can read a text in English (and some other languages as well) and assign appropriate parts of speech tags to each word (such as noun, verb, adjective, adverb). It is also capable of tagging with more sophisticated tags such as noun-singular, noun-plural. Below is an example of a tagged sentence

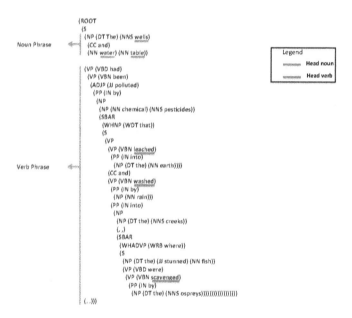

Figure 2.2.1. An example a tagged sentence by Stanford POS Tagger

The sentence that is tagged by the Stanford POS Tagger above is: *The wells and water table had been polluted by chemical pesticides that leached into the earth and washed by rain into the creeks, where the stunned fish were scavenged by the ospreys.* [Matthiessen, 1986]

In this project, we are interested in the top level noun and verb phrase of a sentence, and in particular, the head noun(s) and head verb(s) from the noun and verb phrase respectively. In the above example, *wells*, *water*, and *table* are the head nouns, and *leached*, *washed*, and *scavenged* are the head verbs from the main verb phrase.

2.3 WordNet

Correct meaningful sentences consist of meaningful words. Any system that aims to understand natural language, like humans, must have information about the words and their appropriate meanings. WordNet [Miller, 1995] can be considered as a database of synonym sets, also known as *synsets*. It puts nouns, verbs, adjectives, and adverbs in appropriate *synsets*, where each *synset* represents a particular concept. These *synsets* are then linked based on the semantic relations that determine the concept's definitions. Hence WordNet can be treated as a giant graph of English words (where similar words are clustered together) and can be used to measure semantic similarity and relatedness between a pair of concepts or word senses. We use WordNet heavily in two of our three algorithms to compute sentence similarity.

In WordNet, semantically similar words are clustered into *synsets*, and the distance between two *synsets* is a measure of how the words from both the *synsets* are semantically related. In our thesis we use the *path_similarity()* function provided by *NLTK Toolkit*. Given two words, this method returns a score denoting how the meaning of two words are, based on the shortest path to the first common ancestor in the graph (this is also called is-a hypernym taxonomy).

Figure 2.3.1. An example of WordNet representation

2.4 Word Sense Disambiguation using Personalized Page Rank

In English there are many words that have multiple meanings. Depending on the context, these words take on different senses. Thus, the problem of understanding which meaning is intended becomes very important and is called word sense disambiguation (WSD). For example: The *bank* [DefencePic, 2012, RiverPic, 2012, BankPic, 2012] is about to overflow. This could mean that the edge of the river is about to overflow with water or the financial institution (bank) is so full of people that people are standing outside the main entrance. Another example is the word *lead*,

Page 14 of 64

which can mean *the metal* or *in front of*. In order to solve this problem, Agirre and Soroa [Agirre and Soroa, 2009] developed a tool that implements a graph based WSD algorithm, using the full graph of WordNet efficiently. This tool takes a word to be disambiguated and its part of speech, and returns the offset of where the word is found in the WordNet (or which *synset* the word belong to).

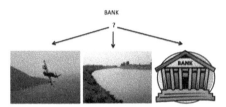

Figure 2.4.1. An example of word sense disambiguation problem

2.5 What is Semantic distance?

Semantic distance is a measure of how close or distant two units of language are in terms of meaning. These units of language can be documents, sentences, phrases, or words. While computing sentence similarity, the unit we are interested is word or term. Two of the algorithms proposed in this project use the idea of semantic distance between words in the same parts of speech from two sentences. Couple of examples about semantic distances between words will help clarify this. The two nouns *dance* [DancePic, 2012] and *choreography* [ChoreographyPic, 2012], for example, are closer in meaning than nouns such as *clown* [ClownPic, 2012] and *cotton* [CottonPic, 2012]. The following figure depicts a very crude representation of the semantic distance between concepts.

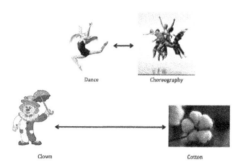

Figure 2.5.1. Example of a semantic distance between concepts

The observation that motivated two of the algorithms proposed in this thesis is that words that are semantically related and semantically similar (e.g synonyms) are much closer to each other in the semantic distance space than words that are only semantically related. For example, carpenter - woodworker is a pair of words that are strongly semantically related and similar, whereas words such as woodworker- chisels are related but not semantically similar. Finally we have words such as chisel - sand which are neither semantically similar nor related in any way.

2.6 Wikipedia and Simple Wikipedia

Articles from Simple English Wikipedia [SimpleWikipedia, 2012] and traditional Wikipedia [Wikipedia, 2012] are the primary data source of this thesis. Simple English Wikipedia articles represent a simplified version of the traditional English Wikipedia articles. There are more than 60,000 articles in the Simple Wikipedia and each of these has its respective *original* version in the traditional Wikipedia. All these articles are written by humans; hence these texts can be considered to be reasonably good aligned documents/articles.

2.7   Semantic Similarity Benchmark Data Sets

One of the most important factors to consider while coming up with good sentence similarity measurement algorithms is the process of evaluation. Due to the complexity of the English language it is hard to find any validated measurements that can be used to judge the performance of the algorithms. Unfortunately, there are not that many human judged sentence pairs out there and only human judged sentence pairs can be considered as the gold standard. Moreover, the process of judging pairs of sentences and assigning a numerical score based on the semantic similarity of the sentence is very expensive and time consuming.

2.7.1 Human judged sentence pairs

When using humans to collect semantic similarity scores for sentence pairs, a particular sentence pair might get different similarity scores from each individuals. This is a very subjective issue, and the only way to overcome this is to have more people evaluate the same sentences and take the average of that. Rubenstein and Goodenough [Li et al., 2006, Rubenstein and Goodenough, 1965, Li et al., Aug] conducted quantitative experiments with human subjects (51 in total) who were asked to rate 65 English word pairs on a scale from 0 to 4 as per their semantic distance. Extending this for his PhD thesis, Jim O'Shea, compiled a set of 65 English sentence pairs which can be treated as a benchmark for validating sentence similarity scores [Li et al., 2006]. He used Rubenstein and Goodenough's word pairs while constructing these sentence pairs. This data set was constructed with human similarity scores provided by 32 participants. Each participant assigned a numerical score, on a scale of 0 to 4, 0 being semantically totally unrelated and 4 being semantically very similar. We used these 65 sentence pairs to evaluate the performance of our algorithms.

2.7.2 SEMILAR: The Semantic Similarity Corpus

This is another corpus of 700 sentence pairs taken from the Microsoft Research Paraphrase Corpus (MSRP). The original purpose of the SEMILAR [Rus et al., 2012] corpus is to provide word-level semantic similarity judgements made by humans which can be used to compute the semantic similarity of larger texts such as sentences and paragraphs. In this thesis, we will treat these sentence pairs as semantically similar sentences, and will evaluate the performance of our algorithms using these sentences. One of the biggest shortcomings of this dataset is that there are no numerical scores assigned to the sentence pairs; hence the notion of semantic relatedness between a pair of sentences here remains arbitrary. We ran our algorithms on this dataset and on a shuffled version of the same dataset, and then compared the similarity scores.

2.8 Correlation and Covariance

In statistics, covariance and correlation together express the degree of similarity between two random variables.

Covariance tells us how two variables are related to each other. Correlation is a measure of the strength of relationship between two random variables, X and Y. In other words, the correlation coefficient summarizes the direction and closeness of linear relations between two variables. The correlation coefficient between two random variables can be computed according to the following formula:

$$corr(X, Y) = \rho(X, Y) = \frac{Cov[X, Y]}{\sqrt{Var[X] \times Var[Y]}} \tag{2.8.1}$$

where

$$Cov[X, Y] = \frac{\sum_{i=1}^{N} (x_i - \bar{x})(y_i - \bar{y})}{N - 1} \tag{2.8.2}$$

and

$$Var[X] = \frac{1}{N-1} \sum_{i=1}^{N} (x - \bar{x}) \tag{2.8.3}$$

The correlation coefficient can take on values from -1 to $+1$. The sign of the correlation indicates the direction of the relationship between the two variables. When the correlation coefficient is positive, it means that as the value of one variable increases, so does the other. On the other hand, if the correlation coefficient is negative, it indicates that when one variable increases, the other variable decreases. If the correlation coefficient is 0 then there is no relationship between the variables.

In order to evaluate the performance of our algorithms, we computed the correlation between the human scores from the O'Shea data and our particular algorithm's sentence similarity scores.

2.9 Related Works

Numerous work has been done on measuring similarity between texts of varying length [Allen, 1987, Hatzivassiloglou et al., 1999, Landauer et al., 1997]. There are a handful works [Li et al., 2006, Mihalcea et al., 2006] relating to the similarity measurement between short texts such as sentences. The primary data in this thesis are articles from Simple Wikipedia and traditional Wikipedia, and we first align paragraphs that are semantically similar using the approach of Kauchak and Coster [Coster and Kauchak, 2011], who worked on aligning paragraphs based on the informations available in the paragraph. They used *tf-idf* weighting to construct vectors representing each paragraph and then compute the cosine similarity between the vectors for finding the similarity score between two paragraphs. We implement their approach for paragraph alignment.

Once paragraphs are aligned, our main goal is to compute cosine similarity between sentences in a pair of aligned paragraphs. Li et al [Li et al., 2006] presented an algorithm for computing sentence similarity that incorporates semantic relatedness and word order information. In addition to using word order similarity, their algorithm weights the semantic distance between words from two sentences with the frequency count of the word in the Brown corpus. This motivated our second algorithm, presented in Section 4.2.2, where we measure sentence similarity by computing semantic similarity between words from the same part of speech. We do not include any word order information in our similarity measurements. In our third algorithm, unlike Li et al, we weight the semantic scores with the *tf-idf* weight of the words. Mihalcea et al [Mihalcea et al., 2006] presented several methods for computing semantic similarity between texts. In one of the algorithms, they weight the word to word similarity scores with the *idf* weight of the words, then they compute the similarity by combining the weights. Our third algorithm differ from Mihalcea et al in that we weight the semantic similarity scores with the *tf-idf* weight whereas they weight by *idf*.

3
Paragraph Alignment

In this project our final goal was to compute semantic similarity between sentence pairs from two given articles or documents. In general, articles consist of one or more paragraphs which in turn contain sentences. Therefore, some form of semantic alignment at paragraph level will make the task of finding similar sentence pairs much easier. In this chapter we will explore how to align paragraphs. For this thesis, the primary source of such document pairs are the articles from Simple Wikipedia and the traditional Wikipedia. Throughout the rest of the thesis, we will refer to article from traditional Wikipedia as *normal* and the corresponding article from Simple Wikipedia as *simple*. Every paragraph from *simple* is aligned with a paragraph from *normal* using *tf-idf* weighting principle [Coster and Kauchak, 2011].

Hence we assume that that there are two versions, A_1, A_2 (one from simple wiki and the other from normal wiki), of the same article written by different authors. It is also assumed that one of the authors conveys the information in a more simplistic manner, preserving the meaning and losing as little relevant information as possible compared to the other author. The long term goal is to quantitatively measure a score between all sentence pair (s_1, s_2) where $s_1 \in A_1$ and $s_2 \in A_2$. But in this chapter, given two documents A_1 and A_2, we focus on aligning paragraphs.

3.1 Why use *tf-idf* weighting scheme?

In this thesis, we use *tf-idf* weighting to align paragraphs and sentences. In order to compute similarity between two unit of languages (could be paragraph or sentences) from statistical point of view, we need to know the frequency count of every word across sentences, paragraphs, and a collection of documents. For example, if a word such as, *squirrel* appears four times in a paragraph (or sentence) against another paragraph (or sentence) where *squirrel* appears only twice, it can be a reasonable conclusion that both the paragraphs (or sentences) can be talking about the same topic, i.e, *squirrel*. But it is not wise to consider that just because *squirrel* appears six times between these two units of languages it must be that these two units are the most semantically similar pairs across the documents. One cannot rule out the possibility that there might be another paragraph (or sentence) which can be a better match. This is where inverse document frequency *idf* becomes helpful. *idf* helps find a numeric measure of the informativeness of a word with respect to the whole document. Hence *tf-idf* can be used to build a statistical map or representation of the words in the paragraphs. Once every word's *tf-idf* weight is known, paragraphs (or sentences) can be represented as vectors, and computing the cosine similarity between the vectors gives a measure of similarity between the paragraphs (or sentences).

3.2 What is the advantage of aligning paragraphs?

Since we are interested in finding sentence similarity between sentences from two articles, why do we care about aligning paragraphs? Why not just pick a sentence from one article and then compare it with every sentences from the other article? This is a very naive approach, also known as the brute force method, and can be computationally very expensive if the article's size is large.

Instead of exhaustively looking for the most similar sentence throughout the entire article, what if we somehow decide where to look to find the most similar sentence? Ideally people use paragraphs to give structure to a piece of writing. Paragraphs can be treated as ways to organize one's thoughts and tell the readers where the idea is going. Hence, for the sake of coherency it is important that one only expresses one idea or set of similar ideas in each paragraph. This led to our intuition of considering articles or texts as a big architecture consisting of smaller architectures. Inside an article, paragraphs are the biggest structures. So if we can pair up paragraphs that are discussing similar ideas, broadly, then we have a better chance of finding similar sentence pairs. Thus, by considering the rules that humans follow when they write, we can not only make the process of sentence alignment faster by aligning paragraphs first but also reduce the computational power required to do the task. However, it is imperative to notice that any inaccurate paragraph alignment will cause inaccurate sentence alignment as well. But the efficiency gain makes this process worthwhile.

3.3   How are paragraphs aligned?

The paragraph alignment process starts with two articles in two separate text files, labeled as *simple* and *normal* from Simple Wikipedia and traditional Wikipedia respectively. The following pseudocode of a helper function that we will later use in the paragraph alignment algorithm.

Algorithm 1 filterWords(P)

Require: A list of paragraphs, P
1: $result \leftarrow [\ ]$
2: **for** p in P **do**
3:      $words \leftarrow$ word_tokenize(p)
4:      **for** w in $words$ **do**
5:          **if** w in STOPWORDS or w in PUNCTLIST **then**
6:              $words$.remove(w)
7:          **end if**
8:      **end for**
9:      **for** w in $words$ **do**
10:         $result$.append(w)
11:     **end for**
12: **end for**
13: **return** $result$

Given a list of paragraphs, the above helper method loops through every paragraphs from the list of paragraphs removes all the extremely common words, also know as *stop words*, and punctuations. It is important to exclude these *stop words* and punctuation because they do not significantly contribute to the meaning of a sentence. The pseudocode for the entire paragraph alignment algorithm is shown below:

Algorithm 2 Paragraph alignment algorithm

Require: 2 articles in separate text files, *simple* and *normal* as input
1: *simpleParas*, *normalParas* ← extractParagraphs(*simple,normal*)
2: *simpleParas*, *normalParas* ← removeSubtitles(*simpleParas*, *normalParas*)
3: *SPara_words* ← filterWords(simpleParas)
4: *NPara_words* ← filterWords(normalParas)
5: *simple_tfidf.txt*, *normal_tfidf.txt* ← compute_tfidf(*SPara_words*, *NPara_words*)
6: *topSWords*, *topNWords* ← extractTopWords(*simple_tfidf.txt*, *normal_tfidf.txt*)
7: *paired paragraphs* ← matchingPara(*topSWords*, *topNWords*)

In line 1 all the paragraphs from both the articles are extracted and stored in separate lists. Since we only care about raw text from the articles, any section titles, subsection titles, etc. are removed so that the system cannot register them as paragraphs. This is done in line 2. In line 3 and 4, we invoke the filterWords() method. At this point we have all the important words from the *simpleParas* and *normalParas* stored in two lists, *SPara_words* and *NPara_words* respectively. The program then computes the *tf-idf* of every word from the two articles. This is done by the compute_tfidf() in line 5. Once all the word's *tf-idf* weights are computed (for the respective paragraphs) the program sorts the words in descending order and saves them, along with the *tf-idf* weight, in separate text files. This is done towards the end of the compute_tfidf() method, right before it returns the tuple *simple_tfidf.txt*, *normal_tfidf.txt*.

The next step is to use these *tf-idf* weights and come up with a correspondence between the paragraphs of the two articles. For every paragraph, the program extracts the top fifteen words with highest *tf-idf* weight. This is done in line 6. Notice, only the top fifteen words are picked because the important meaningful words have larger *tf-idf* weights and are mostly found within the top 15 words. Words beyond these fifteen words seemed to have negligible weights because these words are less informative in forming the main context of the paragraph. The next step would be to use these top fifteen words from the respective paragraphs and compute the paragraph similarity score. This is done by the *matchingPara()* method in line 7. What matchingPara() does is it finds the words (from the the top fifteen) that are common to both the paragraphs and construct two separate vectors V_S and V_N for the paragraphs from *simple* and *normal* respectively. Next, we compute the cosine similarity between V_S and V_N according to the following formula:

$$similarity = cos(\theta) = \frac{V_N.V_S}{||V_N||||V_S||} = \frac{\sum_{i=1}^{n} V_{N_i} \times V_{S_i}}{\sqrt{\sum_{i=1}^{n}(V_{N_i})^2} \times \sqrt{\sum_{i=1}^{n}(V_{S_i})^2}} \quad (3.3.1)$$

Then for every paragraph $p_s \in simple$ a paragraph $p_n \in normal$ with the highest similarity score is found. At the end, the index of which paragraph from *simple* maps to which paragraph from *normal* is obtained and stored in a dictionary. Hence the process of paragraph alignment ends and this is later used in the sentence alignment.

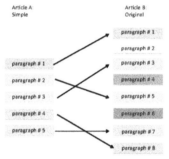

Figure 3.3.1. Example of a paragraph alignment

The following figure depicts the flow of the paragraph alignment program:

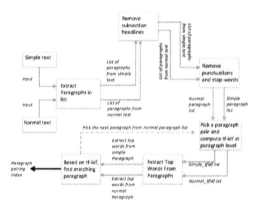

Figure 3.3.2. Flow diagram for paragraph alignment

The table below shows some paragraph alignment results for article on Alan Turing.

Paragraph from Simple Wiki	Paragraph from Traditional Wiki	Alignment info (sim:nor)
Turing was interested in artificial intelligence . He proposed the Turing test , to say when a machine could be called " intelligent ". A computer could be said to " think " if a human interrogator could not tell it apart , through conversation , from a human being.	In 1948 , he was appointed Reader in the Mathematics Department at the University of Manchester . In 1949 , he became Deputy Director of the Computing Laboratory there , working on software for one of the earliest stored - program computersâ ÃT the Manchester Mark 1 . During this time he continued to do more abstract work in mathematics , and in "Computing machinery and intelligence" (Mind , October 1950), Turing addressed the problem of artificial intelligence , and proposed an experiment which became known as the Turing test , an attempt to define a standard for a machine to be called "intelligent". The idea was that a computer could be said to " think " if a human interrogator could not tell it apart , through conversation , from a human being . In the paper , Turing suggested that rather than building a program to simulate the adult mind , it would be better rather to produce a simpler one to simulate a child ' s mind and then to subject it to a course of education . A reversed form of the Turing test is widely used on the Internet ; the CAPTCHA test is intended to determine whether the user is a human or a computer.	2:31
In 1954 , after suffering for two years , he died after eating an apple which was poisoned with cyanide . Or drinking the cyanide in water . The reason for the confusion is that the police never tested the apple for cyanide .	On 8 June 1954 , Turing ' s cleaner found him dead ; he had died the previous day . A post - mortem examination established that the cause of death was cyanide poisoning . When his body was discovered , an apple lay half - eaten beside his bed , and although the apple was not tested for cyanide , it is speculated that this was the means by which a fatal dose was consumed . An inquest determined that he had committed suicide , and he was cremated at Woking Crematorium on 12 June 1954 . Turing ' s ashes were scattered at Woking Crematorium as had been those of his father.	6:39

4
Sentence Alignment

In Chapter 3 we considered an article as a big architecture which contains other smaller structures. In a well written article or a piece of text, paragraphs help in conveying information in a coherent manner by clustering ideas that are similar. Paragraphs consists of sentences; therefore sentences are the next biggest structures inside a paragraph. So far in this thesis, we have discussed how to align paragraphs from two given articles or documents.

The next step is to extract sentence pairs that are semantically similar, given a pair of aligned paragraphs. Meaningful sentences are formed when words are put together in a correct manner. This make words the smallest unit in our architecture framework of articles. For this reason, when similarity between two English sentences are considered, we are essentially looking for words between two sentences that have some semantic similarity (or dissimilarity) between them. Hence it is very natural that our attention goes to the words that are present in the sentences. Given two sentences, one way to start the process of computing sentence similarity is to ask the following questions: how many times does a particular word appears across a pair of sentences? How are the nouns (e.g the subject of a sentence) related to each other in a pair of sentences ? Are they synonyms of each other? Are they semantically related all? How about the actions that the noun undertakes? That is, are there any statistical or semantic similarities between the principle verb(s) and noun(s) in a pair of sentences?

In this chapter, three different algorithms are proposed to compute sentence similarity. The rest of the chapter is laid out as follows: Section 4.1 presents a purely statistical approach to English sentence alignment; Section 4.2 describes a semantic approach; and finally Section 4.3 presents an algorithm that is the combination of the two previous approaches.

4.1   Using term frequency and inverse document frequency *tf-idf*

Given our aligned paragraphs, the next step is to compute sentence similarity between sentences from the two paragraphs. The proposed algorithm is purely statistical. Paragraphs contain sentences; and since we are interested in aligning sentences, paragraphs can be treated as a collection of sentences.

4.1.1 Overview of the Algorithm

From our given aligned paragraph pairs, we pick a pair of aligned paragraphs from the *simple* and *normal* article. From now on, the paragraph from *simple* will be referred as S and the paragraph from *normal* as N. Then we compute the *tf-idf* weight of all the words in S and N. Then for every sentence from S, a sentence from N is chosen and two vectors representing the two sentences are constructed. These vectors are filled with the *tf-idf* weight of the word from the respective paragraphs. Finally the similarity between the sentence pair is found by computing the cosine similarity between the vectors. The program then chooses the next sentence from N and repeats the process. Finally we record the sentence pairs with the highest similarity score.

4.1.2 Pure tf-idf: An algorithm for computing sentence similarity using tf-idf

The sentence alignment process starts by choosing two aligned paragraphs from *simple* and *normal* articles. This technique of computing sentence similarity is a well known algorithm in the NLP community [Salton and Buckley, 1988, Wu and Salton, 1981]. The following is the pseudocode of a helper function that we invoke several times in our sentence similarity algorithm.

Algorithm 3 computeTfidf(P, Col)

Require: (a) A paragraph, P. (b) Collection of all the word form P.
1: $Words \leftarrow [\ ]$
2: **for** *sentence* in P **do**
3:    **for** *term* in *sentence* **do**
4:       **if** *term* is not PUNCTLIST, STOPWORDS, commonAuxilaryVerbs **then**
5:          $weight \leftarrow Col.\text{tf\_idf}(term, sentence)$
6:          $w = \text{Word}(term)$ {this is a Word Object}
7:          $Words.\text{append}(w.\text{setWeight}(weight))$
8:       **end if**
9:    **end for**
10: **end for**
11: **return** $Words$

Given a paragraph P, the above method computes all the word's *tf-idf* weight. It is important to note that line 4 filters out the punctuation, *stop-words* and auxiliary verbs while computing *td-idf* weights. This is because punctuation and *stop-words* are responsible for the structure and organization of written language, whereas auxiliary verbs primarily contribute to constructing a grammatically correct sentence. Generally, none of these words play the major role in forming the core meaning of the sentence. Hence these words can be ignored without losing any important content or information. So we end up computing the *tf-idf* weight of verbs, nouns, adverbs, and adjectives. Notice that these are the words that primarily shape the meaning of a sentence. At the end, the method returns a list of word objects, along with the tf-idf weights.

The pseudocode for the sentence alignment algorithm using *tf-idf* is shown below:

Algorithm 4 Sentence alignment using tf-idf

Require: (a) A dictionary, *pairedPara*, of paragraph pairing indices. (b)Two list of paragraphs simpleParas and normalParas from *simple* and *normal* articles respectively.

1: **for** $sIdx$, $nIdx$ in pairedPara **do**
2:     $S \leftarrow$ simpleParas[$sIdx$]; $N \leftarrow$ normalParas[$nIdx$]
3:     $Words_n$, $Words_n \leftarrow$ extractWords(S, N)
4:     $Col_s \leftarrow$ TextCollection($Words_s$); $Col_n \leftarrow$ TextCollection($Words_n$)
5:     $Words \leftarrow [\ ]$
      {// compute tf-idf weight of words from S and N}
6:     $Words \leftarrow$ computeTfidf(S, Col_s) + computeTfidf(N, Col_n)
7:     **for** s in S **do**
8:       **for** n in N **do**
9:         $U \leftarrow$ Union(s,n)
10:        $V_s \leftarrow [\ ]$; $V_n \leftarrow [\ ]$
11:        **for** *term* in U **do**
12:           $weight_s \leftarrow$ computeWeight(term, s, Words)
13:           $weight_n \leftarrow$ computeWeight(term, n, Words)
14:           V_s.append($weight_s$); V_n.append($weight_n$)
15:        **end for**
16:        $similarity \leftarrow$ computeSimilarity(V_s,V_n) {**SIMILARITY SCORE**}
17:       **end for**
18:     **end for**
19: **end for**

The algorithm starts by selecting a pair of aligned paragraphs S and N in line 2. In line 3, the algorithm extracts all the words from both the paragraphs in two separate lists $Words_s$ and $Words_n$. Then the algorithm produces two separate collection of words, Col_s and Col_n, from $Words_s$ and $Words_n$ respectively. Next, we invoke the computeTfidf() method on S and N separately. The method returns a list of words with *tf-idf* weights. This happens in line 6 and at this point all the word's *tf-idf* weight is known.

Then for every sentence s in S a sentence n from N is selected. These sentences are then joined to get a union U of all the words from both s and s. The purpose of creating a set such as U is to generate two vectors V_s and V_n in $|U| \times 1$ dimensions where V_s in the vector representing s, and V_n is the vector representing the sentence, n. Every entry in each of the vectors is the *tf-idf* weight of a word from U. If a particular word or term is not in s or n then that word's weight in the vector is assigned a value of 0. Then the cosine similarity between the two vectors, V_s and V_n is computed using the following formula:

$$similarity - \frac{\sum_{i=1}^{|V_n|} V_{s_i} V_{n_i}}{||V_s|| ||V_n||} \qquad (4.1.1)$$

Since our sentences are represented by vectors, the angle between these vectors is a measure of similarity between two vectors. The similarity score is in the range from 0 to 1. A similarity score of 0 represents that the two sentences are not similar at all, whereas a score of 1 implies that the sentences are very similar (in fact if the sentences have exactly the same content words, they score 1) to each other. Once a similarity score is obtained between sentences s and n, the program loops through every sentence from N and records the maximum similarity score.

The following flow diagram depicts a detailed representation of how the program works:

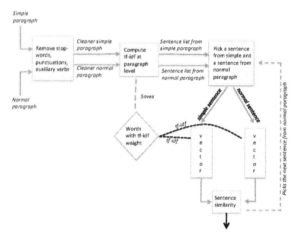

Figure 4.1.1. The flow diagram of the tf-idf algorithm

4.2   Using semantic only

This section proposes another algorithmic approach for computing semantic similarity between English sentence pairs. Unlike the algorithm in Section 4.1, this algorithm is purely based on the semantic distance between the words of two sentences. No statistics are involved in this process. This algorithm uses the semantic relationship between words in order to measure sentence similarity.

4.2.1 Overview of the algorithm

The structure of a correct English sentence consists of at least two main phrases, namely a noun phrase and a verb phrase. Generally the noun phrase contains the subject or topic of the sentence, whereas the verb phrase represents the principle action(s) carried out by the subject. But in reality, the noun phrase and verb phrase may contain other phrases such as prepositional phrases and adjectival phrases. No matter how complex the top level noun phrase and verb phrase are, these phrases contain at least one important noun and verb. These nouns and verbs are called the *head words* of the noun and verb phrases. This observation led to the core idea of the algorithm proposed in this section. Given two sentences, the idea is to extract the head noun(s) and verb(s) from the respective noun and verb phrases and use the semantic distance scores between words of the same part of speech for computing sentence similarity.

4.2.2 Semantic: An algorithm for computing sentence similarity using only semantic distance

Following on Chapter 3, this algorithm starts with the assumption that paragraphs are aligned.

The pseudocode for the entire process is shown below.

Algorithm 5 Sentence alignment algorithm using semantic distance

---

Require: (a) A dictionary, pairedPara, of paragraph pairing indices. (b)Two list of paragraphs simpleParas and normalParas from *simple* and *normal* articles respectively.

```
 1: for sIdx, nIdx in pairedPara do
 2:     S ← simpleParas[sIdx]; N ← normalParas[nIdx]
 3:     for s in S do
 4:         tagged_s ← parse(s)
 5:         for n in N do
 6:             tagged_n ← parse(n)
 7:             N_s, V_s, N_n, V_n ← buildClause(tagged_s, tagged_n)
 8:             noun_s, verb_s, noun_n, verb_n ← extractContext(N_s, V_s, N_n, V_n)
 9:             maxSim_nouns ← [ ]; maxSim_verbs ← [ ]
                {// semantic similarity for nouns}
10:             for n_s in noun_s do
11:                 tempMax ← 0
12:                 for n_n in noun_n do
13:                     sim_score ← n_s.path_similarity(n_n)
14:                     if sim_score > tempMax then
15:                         tempMax ← sim_score
16:                         maxSim_nouns.append(tempMax)
17:                     end if
18:                 end for
19:             end for
                {// semantic similarity for verbs}
20:             for v_s in verb_s do
21:                 tempMax ← 0
22:                 for v_n in verb_n do
23:                     sim_score ← v_s.path_similarity(v_n)
24:                     if sim_score > tempMax then
25:                         tempMax ← sim_score
26:                         maxSim_verbs.append(tempMax)
27:                     end if
28:                 end for
29:             end for
30:             Similarity ← combineSemtanticDistances(maxSim_nouns, maxSim_verbs)
31:         end for
32:     end for
33: end for
```

After extracting a pair of aligned paragraphs S and N in line 2, the program picks a sentence s from S and a sentence n from N and tags the part of speech (POS) of every word in s and in n. The POS tagging is done in line 4 and 6. In line 7, the buildClause() method extracts the top level noun and verb phrases and returns all the head noun(s) and verb(s) from the respective sentence pairs in four separate lists $N_s, V_s, N_n,$ and V_n. Notice, N_s and V_s contains noun(s) and verb(s) from s and N_n and V_n contains noun(s) and verb(s) from n . extractContext( ) function, in line 8, works on the lists of noun(s) and verb(s) from line 7 and finds in which *synset* the words belong to in the WordNet. At this point, we have all the information required to compute the semantic distance between the words from the same POS. In lines 10 to 19, the semantic similarity between every noun from s and n is computed and the length of shortest path that connects the senses between two nouns in the is-a hypernym taxonomy is found and saved. Similarly the semantic distance between the verbs from the two sentences are also found between lines 20 and 29. At this point, the similarity score between sentence s and n is computed by adding all the semantic distance measures between the nouns and verbs from the respective sentences. Suppose S_k and S_l are two sentences, the sentence similarity between two sentences is computed according to the following formula:

$$Semantic\ similarity(S_k, S_l) = \sum_{i=1}^{N} maxSim(n_i \leftrightarrow n_j) + \sum_{i=1}^{V} maxSim(v_i \leftrightarrow v_m) \qquad (4.2.1)$$

where, $j \geq 1$, N = number of nouns in S_k, V = number of verbs in S_k, $v_i \leftrightarrow v_j$ is the semantic similarity between the ith verb from sentence S_k and m^{th} verb from S_l, and $n_i \leftrightarrow n_j$ is the semantic similarity between the ith noun from S_k and j^{th} noun from S_l.

Figure 4.2.1 represents a pictorial representation of the above formula for the example sentence from Section 2.2 with an arbitrary sentence. Then Figure 4.2.2 presents a detailed flow diagram of the process involved in computing the semantic similarity between sentences

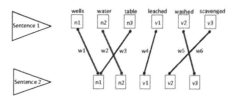

Semantic Similarity(Sentence1, Sentence 2) = w1 + w2 + w3 + w4 + w5 + w6

Figure 4.2.1. Computing sentence similarity using the Semantic algorithm

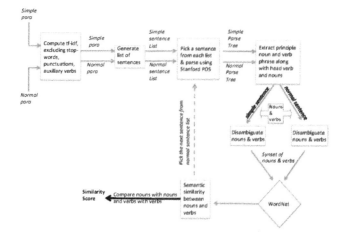

Figure 4.2.2. The flow diagram of the Semantic algorithm

4.3   Using both semantic distance and *tf-idf*

So far we have explored algorithms that are either purely statistical or semantic in nature. The goal in this section was to come up with an algorithm that incorporated both semantic and statistical information. The algorithm that is proposed is the combination of the algorithms in Section 4.1 and Section 4.2. After computing all the *tf-idf* weights of every word in paragraphs, the idea is to use these scores to assign weight to the semantic distance measures between words of same part of speech (nouns and verbs only) in the sentences. Finally we use these weighted scores to compute the semantic similarity between sentence pairs.

4.3.1 Combined: An algorithm for computing sentence similarity using tf-idf and semantic distance scores

The algorithm starts with a given pair of aligned paragraphs. The pseudocode for this algorithms

is shown in the next page.

Algorithm 6 Sentence alignment algorithm using semantic distance and *tf-idf*

Require: (a) A dictionary, pairedPara, of paragraph pairing indices. (b)Two list of paragraphs simpleParas and normalParas from *simple* and *normal* articles respectively.

1: **for** $sIdx$, $nIdx$ in pairedPara **do**
2:    $S \leftarrow$ simpleParas$[sIdx]$; $N \leftarrow$ normalParas$[nIdx]$
3:    $allWords \leftarrow$ Execute Algorithm 4 up to line 6
4:    **for** s in S **do**
5:       **for** n in N **do**
6:          ss_{words}, $ns_{words} \leftarrow$ Execute Algorithm 5 up to line 29 for s and n
7:          $nume_A$, $nume_B$, $denom_A$, $denom_B \leftarrow 0$
8:          **for** $word$ in ss_{words} **do**
9:             $tfidf \leftarrow allWords[word.getValue()]$
10:            $semanticWeight \leftarrow word.getWeight()$
11:            $nume_A \leftarrow nume_A + (semanticWeight * tfidf)$
12:            $denom_A \leftarrow denom_A + allWords[word.getValue()]$
13:         **end for**
14:         $partA \leftarrow \frac{nume_A}{denom_A}$
15:         **for** $word$ in ss_{words} **do**
16:            $tfidf \leftarrow allWords[word.getValue()]$
17:            $semanticWeight \leftarrow word.getWeight()$
18:            $nume_B \leftarrow nume_B + (semanticWeight \times tfidf)$
19:            $denom_B \leftarrow denom_B + allWords[word.getValue()]$
20:         **end for**
21:         $partB \leftarrow \frac{nume_B}{denom_B}$
22:         **Similarity Score** $\leftarrow \frac{1}{2}(partA + partB)$
23:      **end for**
24:   **end for**
25: **end for**

The algorithm starts by choosing an aligned pair of paragraphs, S and N, in line 2. Then the *tf-idf* weight of every word in S and N is computed in line 3 and is later used in weighting the semantic distance scores. This ends the statistical part of this algorithm.

The next step of the program is to compute the semantic part of the algorithm. Given two sentences s and n from S and N respectively, a part of the algorithm proposed in Section 4.2.2 is carried out in order to find the semantic distance between all the noun(s) and verb(s) from s with the noun(s) and verb(s) from n. This is done at line 6. At this point, the lists ss_{words} and ns_{words} contain all the noun(s) and verb(s), along with the semantic similarity scores, from s and n, respectively.

Once all the semantic distance measures between the nouns and verbs from s and the corresponding nouns and verbs from n are computed, the semantic distance scores are weighted with the *tf-idf* weight of the nouns and verbs from s. Then the process is repeated, but this time the semantic distances between the nouns and verbs from n and the nouns and verbs from s are computed and weighted based on the *tf-idf* scores of the nouns and verbs from n. At this point all the information required to compute the sentence similarity between the two sentences s and n are obtained and can be formulated according to the following equation:

$$sim_{tfidf,\ sem}(s,n) = \frac{1}{2}\left(\frac{\sum_{w \in s} maxSim(w,n) \times \textit{tf-idf}(w)}{\sum_{w \in s} \textit{tf-idf}(w)}\right. \tag{4.3.1}$$
$$+$$
$$\left.\frac{\sum_{w \in n} maxSim(w,s) \times \textit{tf-idf}(w)}{\sum_{w \in n} \textit{tf-idf}(w)}\right)$$

where *maxSim(w,n)* is the maximum semantic similarity score of w and the words in n that belong to the same part of speech as w. Same idea holds for *maxSim(w,s)*. *tf-idf(w)* is the inverse document frequency weight of w. Semantic similarity scores are computed between words from same parts of speech because WordNet cannot compute the semantic distance of the cross part of speech words. The statistical importance of a word is determined using the *tf-idf* weight. The word similarities are weighted with the corresponding word informativeness (*tf-idf* weights), summed and normalized by the *tf-idf* scores. Finally, the semantic similarity score is computed by taking the simple average. This algorithm is an extension of the algorithm proposed in [Mihalcea et al., 2006], and the difference is that in the paper, they weight semantic scores by the *idf* weight of the word.

The figure below is the detailed flow diagram of the process involved in computing the semantic similarity between sentences using *tf-idf* and semantic distance between words:

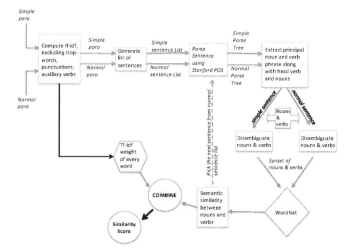

Figure 4.3.1. The flow diagram of the Combined algorithm

5
Evaluation

So far we have explored three different approaches to computing English sentence similarity. The work remains incomplete if we do not have any assessment of how the algorithms perform with a set of sentence pairs of known semantic similarity. We will use O'Shea's 65 sentence pair dataset and the SEMILAR dataset, discussed in Section 2.7, to evaluate the performance of our algorithms. For every sentence pair from O'Shea's dataset, the goal is to compare sentence similarity scores from the respective algorithms with the human assigned scores. The SEMILAR dataset is used to investigate the responsiveness of the respective algorithms to known semantically similar/dissimilar sentence pairs as input. For simplicity, from now on, the algorithm from Section 4.2 will be called Semantic and the algorithm from Section 4.3 will be Combined.

5.1   Using O'Shea's 65 Sentence Pairs:

O'Shea compiled 65 human judged sentence pairs for his PhD thesis [Li et al., Aug], and we will use these sentence pairs to evaluate the performance of our algorithms. We will compute the sentence similarity for every sentence pair from the dataset using both the **Semantic** and **Combined** algorithms and compare these similarity scores with the human judged scores. Thus we can evaluate the performance of our algorithms.

After computing the sentence similarity scores for both **Semantic** and **Combined** algorithms, every pair of sentences is represented by an (X, Y) tuple where X is the human judged score and Y represents the similarity score from a particular algorithm. Both X and Y are considered as independent random variables and we compute the correlation between X and Y. Correlation measure will help us understand how much change in human score, X, is detected by the algorithm's score, Y. The table in the Appendix shows the sentence pairs with their corresponding scores from the respective algorithms.

Once we have the semantic similarity scores, a scatter plot of human scores vs the algorithm scores for all the 65 sentence pair can be constructed which will show a more clear picture regarding the performance of our algorithms. The following graphs depict the scatter plot of the **Semantic** and **Combined** respectively.

Ideally we want all the data points to lie on the $y = x$ line for both the graphs. This would mean that both the human score and the algorithm's similarity score are exactly equal, meaning our algorithm matches humans in assessing sentence pairs. Remember that X and Y are independent of each other; in other words, human assigned scores do not affect the algorithm's output similarity score. Realistically we want the human score and the algorithm similarity score to be as close as possible. The following table depicts the correlation and covariance between the random vari-

Scatter Plot for Semantic algorithm

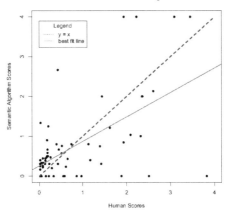

Figure 5.1.1. Scatter plot for Semantic algorithm

able X (the known human scores) and Y (the algorithm output) for both Semantic and Combined :

Algorithms	σ_Y	σ_X	Cov[X,Y]	r = Corr[X,Y]
Semantic	1.021	0.970	0.5789	0.5890
Combined	1.031	0.970	0.6910	0.6899

Table 5.1: Sentence similarity correlation comparison between Semantic and Combined

From the above table we see that the correlation coefficient r is greater than 0 for both the algorithms, which means that the two variables increase together. In fact, the difference of 0.1009 in correlation is quite significant, showing that Combined algorithm is better than Sementic. Moreover, the slope of the best fit line for the Combined algorithm is more closer to the slope of $y = x$ line than the Semantic.

Another way to notice the difference in performance of the Semantic and Combined algorithm is to measure the mean absolute difference between the algorithm's similarity score and the human score. The mean absolute difference is less interesting than the correlation, and will not help us make any stronger conclusion. The smaller the mean absolute difference, the better (that is, the

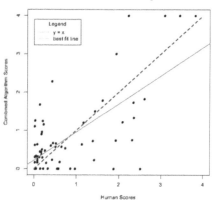

Figure 5.1.2. Scatter plot for Combined algorithm

closer the algorithm's score is to human score). The following table depicts the mean absolute

difference in score for Semantic and Combined algorithms with human score.

Algorithms	Mean absolute difference from human score
Semantic	0.5908
Combined	0.5621

Table 5.2: Average mean difference from human score for each algorithm

We can see that the mean differences for the two algorithms is roughly 0.03. The difference is very

small and does not provide any additional insight about the two algorithm's performance.

5.2   Microsoft Paraphrase

In this section we will investigate how well our algorithms perform on the SEMILAR

[Rus et al., 2012] paraphrase pairs and a scrambled version of SEMILAR. The SEMILAR dataset

has 700 sentence pairs. Every sentence pair consists of two sentences that are paraphrases of each

other. We consider these sentences as already aligned semantically similar sentence pairs, and compute their similarity scores. Our next step is to make some controlled change in the SEMILAR sentence pairs and investigate how our algorithms respond to this change. So we scramble the second sentence of all the 700 sentence pairs, making the sentence pairs no longer a good aligned sentence pair. From now on, this rearranged sentence pairs will be referred as Shuffled dataset and the original SEMILAR paraphrase pairs as the Original dataset. The next step is to compute the sentence similarity score for the Shuffled sentence pairs and compare the scores with the scores from the Original dataset. Note that we expect pairs in the Original dataset to be highly similar and pairs in the Shuffled dataset to be dissimilar. The following table depicts the result of running the Semantic algorithm and Combined algorithm on the Original and Shuffled dataset.

Algorithms	$N_{Or < Sh}$	$N_{Or = Sh}$	$N_{Or > Sh}$	$Mean_{Or}$	$Mean_{Sh}$	$Mean_{dif}$
Semantic	138	35	527	1.60	0.50	1.33
Combined	134	20	546	2.40	1.10	1.63

Table 5.3: Semantic and Combined algorithm's result on both Original and Shuffled.

where,

- $N_{Or < Sh}$: number of sentence pairs where similarity score from Original dataset < similarity score from Shuffled dataset

- $N_{Or = Sh}$: number of sentence pairs where similarity score from Original dataset = similarity score from Shuffled dataset.

- $N_{Or > Sh}$: number of sentence pairs where similarity score from Original dataset > similarity score from Shuffled dataset.

- $Mean_{Or}$: Mean similarity score of Original dataset

- $Mean_{Sh}$: Mean similarity score of Shuffled dataset

- $Mean_{dif}$: Mean difference in similarity score between `Original` and `Shuffled`

Since `Combined` is the most complicated algorithm here, we hope that `Combined` algorithm's performance will be better than `Semantic` algorithm. This expectation is supported by the fourth column of the table which shows that out of the 700 sentence pairs `Combined` algorithm found more sentences that are semantically similar to each other than `Semantic` algorithm. Ideally, we want both of our algorithms to label all 700 sentence pairs to be semantically similar.

Another way to access the two algorithms is to check how well the algorithms distinguish good aligned pairs from bad (pair from `Shuffled`). The value of $Mean_{Or}$ - $Mean_{Sh}$ is a measure of how well the algorithms can classify sentence pairs. For `Semantic`, this difference is 1.1 and for `Combined` the difference is 1.3. This difference of 0.2 is not that large, but it is an indication that `Combined` can be more promising in distinguishing between good and bad sentence pairs than `Semantic`. Ideally we want this difference to be as close as possible to 4.

However, the $Mean_{Sh}$ column in the table suggests that `Combined` is not necessarily always a better algorithm than `Semantic`. This is because the average similarity score for `Semantic` on the `Shuffled` dataset is less than half the mean similarity score by `Combined` algorithm. This implies that, overall, `Semantic` did a better job than the `Combined` on the `Shuffled` dataset. This also raises the concern that perhaps `Combined` algorithm always gives high score to a sentence pair, irrespective of whether it is semantically similar or not.

After shuffling, `Combined` algorithm recognizes 134 sentence pairs as semantically similar. On the contrary, `Semantic` recognizes 138 sentence pairs as semantically similar. This is a very small distinction and does not provide any additional concrete fact to our understanding of the two algorithms.

Ideally, after shuffling, the similarity score for the majority of the sentence pairs should change, and in particular should decrease for both the algorithms. But, for SEMILAR, the similarity scores do not reflect that, and hence we can not make any conclusion about which algorithm is better. However, we noticed that, after shuffling, `Combined` algorithm is slightly more responsive to the change than the Semantic. This is suggested by the $N_{Or\ =\ Sh}$ column of the table which suggests that there are fewer sentence pairs (20 vs 35) whose similarity scores remained unaffected.

Finally, we plot the sentence similarity score distribution for both the Semantic and the Combined algorithm. The histograms presents a pictorial summary of the two algorithm's application on the Original and Shuffled dataset.

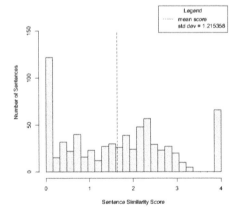

Figure 5.2.1. Similarity score distribution for Semantic algorithm on Original

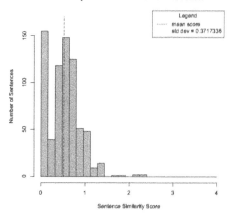

Figure 5.2.2. Similarity score distribution for Semantic algorithm on Shuffled

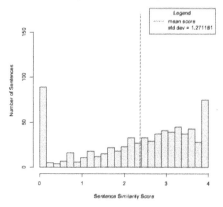

Figure 5.2.3. Similarity score distribution for Combined algorithm on Original

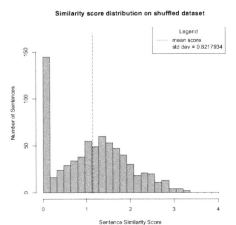

Figure 5.2.4. Similarity score distribution for Combined algorithm on Shuffled

In the above similarity score distributions, it is noticed that both the algorithms are quite good at detecting changes to the Original dataset. For both the algorithms, we expected the mean similarity score on the Original dataset to be approximately around or between 3 and 4. But we found the mean similarity scores to be between 1.5 to 2.5 (the dotted vertical line in Figure 5.2.1 and 5.2.3). After shuffling, we expected the scores to drop significantly, and this is reflected by the low mean score in Figure 5.2.2 and 5.2.4.

6
Discussion

The objective of this project was to explore ways to compute English sentence similarity. Having a good algorithm for measuring sentence similarity will enable us to produce a large corpus of aligned sentence pairs which could be used to build a language knowledge database for existing Information Retrieval (IR) systems such as the Google, Yahoo. We presented three algorithms: one statistical, one purely semantic and one that combines both the statistical and semantic approaches. The first algorithm uses the vector-space model where every entry of the vector is the *tf-idf* weight of a particular term/word. The second algorithm, Semantic, uses semantic similarity and relatedness measures between words from two sentences for computing the similarity score. The third algorithm, Combined, combines the first and second algorithm by weighting the semantic similarity scores between words with the *tf-idf* weights of the words. We then evaluated the performance of the Semantic and Combined algorithms against human judged sentence pairs and the Microsoft SEMILAR dataset of paraphrase sentence pairs.

The sentence similarity scores from the Combined algorithm were closer to the human judged scores than the Semantic algorithm's scores, as reflected by the correlation value of 0.68 for Combined vs 0.58 for Semantic. This encouraged us to explore whether the Combined algorithm is always better than the `Semantic` algorithm, using the sentence pairs from the SEMILAR dataset. These sentence pairs do not have any numeric score representing their semantic similarity. However, since the sentence pairs are paraphrases of each other, we expect the similarity score for these sentence pairs to be quite high. We then made a controlled change to the SEMILAR dataset by shuffling the sentence pairs, which should give low similarity scores overall. We found that the difference in mean similarity score between the bad and good sentence pairs for `Combined` was larger than the difference in mean similarity score between good and bad sentence pairs for `Semantic`, which suggested that `Combined` did a better job in distinguishing between good and bad sentence pairs `than Semantic`.

Notice that we do not evaluate the first algorithm in Section 4.1. This is because when we compute sentence similarity between two sentences, we treat a single sentence as a document, and the *idf* component of a word becomes zero. Hence the *tf-idf* score also becomes zero. Moreover, it is important to note that we do not evaluate the accuracy of our paragraph alignment algorithm. Even if some alignments are incorrect, the efficiency gain is worthwhile.

One limitation of our approach is that we assume that the lexical database of WordNet contains most of the English words, but this is not the case. There are many words such as proper names and derivative words that are not included in WordNet. Therefore whenever we have such words in sentence pairs, our WordNet queries fail to return a word similarity score, and we set the semantic similarity score for these words to be 0. For this reason, many of our sentence similarity scores are zero.

One of the biggest limitations in this project was that the O'Shea's dataset used in our evaluation contains only 65 human judged sentence pairs. If there were more human judged sentence pairs, we could have evaluated the algorithms to a greater depth, and understood the nature of the proposed algorithms more thoroughly which might have provided us more evidence to make a more definitive conclusion about which algorithm is better. Having said that, the long term goal of this project is to help construct a large corpus of aligned sentence pairs that can be used as the training set for various IR systems, and these algorithms, and in particular Combined algorithm do show some promise.

7
Appendix

Sentence pair	Human Score	Semantic	Combined
Cord is strong, thick string. A smile is the expression that you have on your face when you are pleased or amused, or when you are being friendly.	0.04	0	0
A rooster is an adult male chicken. A voyage is a long journey on a ship or in a spacecraft.	0.02	0.16	0.16
Noon is 12 o'clock in the middle of the day. String is thin rope made of twisted threads, used for tying things together or tying up parcels.	0.05	0	0
Fruit or a fruit is something which grows on a tree or bush and which contains seeds or a stone covered by a substance that you can eat. A furnace is a container or enclosed space in which a very hot fire is made, for example to melt metal, burn rubbish or produce steam.	0.19	0.58	0.96
An autograph is the signature of someone famous which is specially written for a fan to keep. The shores or shore of a sea, lake or wide river is the land along the edge of it.	0.02	0.4	0.62
An automobile is a car. In legends and fairy stories, a wizard is a man who has magic powers.	0.08	0.22	0.22

A mound of something is a large rounded pile of it. A stove is a piece of equipment which provides heat, either for cooking or for heating a room.	0.02	0.25	1.10
A grin is a broad smile. An implement is a tool or other piece of equipment.	0.02	0.30	0.30
An Asylum is a psychiatric hospital. Fruit or a fruit is something which grows on a tree or bush and which contains seeds or a stone covered by a substance that you can eat.	0.02	0	0
An Asylum is a psychiatric hospital. A monk is a member of a male religious community that is usually separated from the outside world.	0.15	0	0
A graveyard is an area of land, sometimes near a church, where dead people are buried. If you describe a place or situation as a madhouse you mean that it is full of confusion and noise.	0.09	0.33	0.31
Glass is a hard transparent substance that is used to make things such as windows and bottles. A magician is a person who entertains people by doing magic tricks.	0.03	1.33	1.25
A boy is a child who will grow up to be a man. A rooster is an adult male chicken.	0.43	0.31	0.23
A cushion is a fabric case filled with soft material, which you put on a seat to make it more comfortable. A jewel is a precious stone used to decorate valuable things that you wear, such as rings or necklaces.	0.21	1.24	1.24
A monk is a member of a male religious community that is usually separated from the outside world. A slave is someone who is the property of another person and has to work for that person.	0.18	0.9	0.9
An Asylum is a psychiatric hospital. A cemetery is a place where dead people's bodies or their ashes are buried.	0.15	0	0
The coast is an area of land that is next to the sea. A forest is a large area where trees grow close together.	0.19	0.33	0.5
A grin is a broad smile. A lad is a young man or boy.	0.05	0.21	0.33
The shores or shore of a sea, lake or wide river is the land along the edge of it. Woodland is land with a lot of trees.	0.33	0	0
A monk is a member of a male religious community that is usually separated from the outside world. In ancient times, an oracle was a priest or priestess who made statements about future events or about the truth.	0.45	0.66	0.66

A boy is a child who will grow up to be a man. A sage is a person who is regarded as being very wise.	0.17	0.47	0.43
An automobile is a car. A cushion is a fabric case filled with soft material, which you put on a seat to make it more comfortable.	0.08	0.44	0.27
A mound of something is a large rounded pile of it. The shores or shore of a sea, lake or wide river is the land along the edge of it.	0.14	0.44	1.67
A lad is a young man or boy. In legends and fairy stories, a wizard is a man who has magic powers.	0.13	0.30	0.31
A forest is a large area where trees grow close together. A graveyard is an area of land, sometimes near a church, where dead people are buried.	0.26	0.47	0.47
Food is what people and animals eat. A rooster is an adult male chicken.	0.22	0	0
A cemetery is a place where dead people's bodies or their ashes are buried. Woodland is land with a lot of trees.	0.15	0	0
The shores or shore of a sea, lake or wide river is the land along the edge of it. A voyage is a long journey on a ship or in a spacecraft.	0.08	0.25	0.63
A bird is a creature with feathers and wings, females lay eggs and most birds can fly. Woodland is land with a lot of trees.	0.05	0	0
The coast is an area of land that is next to the sea. A hill is an area of land that is higher than the land that surrounds it.	0.4	0.8	0.6
A furnace is a container or enclosed space in which a very hot fire is made, for example to melt metal, burn rubbish or produce steam. An implement is a tool or other piece of equipment.	0.2	0.5	0.29
A crane is a large machine that moves heavy things by lifting them in the air. A rooster is an adult male chicken.	0.08	0.25	0.16
A hill is an area of land that is higher than the land that surrounds it. Woodland is land with a lot of trees.	0.58	0	0
A car is a motor vehicle with room for a small number of passengers. When you make a journey, you travel from one place to another.	0.29	0.2	0.15
A cemetery is a place where dead people's bodies or their ashes are buried. A mound of something is a large rounded pile of it.	0.23	0.307	1.15

Glass is a hard transparent substance that is used to make things such as windows and bottles. A jewel is a precious stone used to decorate valuable things that you wear, such as rings or necklaces.	0.43	2.66	2.28
A magician is a person who entertains people by doing magic tricks. In ancient times, an oracle was a priest or priestess who made statements about future events or about the truth.	0.52	0.75	0.65
A crane is a large machine that moves heavy things by lifting them in the air. An implement is a tool or other piece of equipment.	0.74	0.8	0.53
Your brother is a boy or a man who has the same parents as you. A lad is a young man or boy.	0.51	0.57	0.57
A sage is a person who is regarded as being very wise. In legends and fairy stories, a wizard is a man who has magic powers.	0.61	0.23	0.17
In ancient times, an oracle was a priest or priestess who made statements about future events or about the truth. A sage is a person who is regarded as being very wise.	1.13	0.8	0.63
A bird is a creature with feathers and wings, females lay eggs and most birds can fly. A crane is a large machine that moves heavy things by lifting them in the air.	0.14	0.38	0.45
A bird is a creature with feathers and wings, females lay eggs and most birds can fly. A cock is an adult male chicken.	0.65	0.43	0.57
Food is what people and animals eat. Fruit or a fruit is something which grows on a tree or bush and which contains seeds or a stone covered by a substance that you can eat.	0.97	0	0
Your brother is a boy or a man who has the same parents as you. A monk is a member of a male religious community that is usually separated from the outside world.	0.18	0.5	0.375
An Asylum is a psychiatric hospital. If you describe a place or situation as a madhouse you mean that it is full of confusion and noise.	0.86	0	0
A furnace is a container or enclosed space in which a very hot fire is made, for example to melt metal, burn rubbish or produce steam. A stove is a piece of equipment which provides heat, either for cooking or for heating a room.	1.39	0.75	0.72
A magician is a person who entertains people by doing magic tricks. In legends and fairy stories, a wizard is a man who has magic powers	1.42	0.31	0.26
A hill is an area of land that is higher than the land that surrounds it. A mound of something is a large rounded pile of it.	1.17	0.4	1.2

Definition pair			
Cord is strong, thick string. String is thin rope made of twisted threads, used for tying things together or tying up parcels.	1.88	0	0
Glass is a hard transparent substance that is used to make things such as windows and bottles. A tumbler is a drinking glass with straight sides.	0.55	0	0
A grin is a broad smile. A smile is the expression that you have on your face when you are pleased or amused, or when you are being friendly.	1.94	4.0	3.0
In former times, serfs were a class of people who had to work on a particular person's land and could not leave without that person's permission. A slave is someone who is the property of another person and has to work for that person.	1.93	0.84	0.74
A When you make a journey, you travel from one place to another. A voyage is a long journey on a ship or in a spacecraft.	1.44	2.0	1.5
An autograph is the signature of someone famous which is specially written for a fan to keep. Your signature is your name, written in your own characteristic way, often at the end of a document to indicate that you wrote the document or that you agree with what it says.	1.62	1.21	1.78
The coast is an area of land that is next to the sea. The shores or shore of a sea, lake or wide river is the land along the edge of it.	2.35	2.0	1.73
A forest is a large area where trees grow close together. Woodland is land with a lot of trees.	2.51	0	0
An implement is a tool or other piece of equipment. A tool is any instrument or simple piece of equipment that you hold in your hands and use to do a particular kind of work.	2.36	2.0	1.33
A cock is an adult male chicken. A rooster is an adult male chicken.	3.45	4.0	4.0
A boy is a child who will grow up to be a man. A lad is a young man or boy.	2.32	1.0	0.75
A cushion is a fabric case filled with soft material, which you put on a seat to make it more comfortable. A pillow is a rectangular cushion which you rest your head on when you are in bed.	2.09	1.03	1.22
A cemetery is a place where dead people's bodies or their ashes are buried. A graveyard is an area of land, sometimes near a church, where dead people are buried.	3.09	4.0	4.0
An automobile is a car. A car is a motor vehicle with room for a small number of passengers.	2.23	4.0	4.0

Midday is 12 o'clock in the middle of the day. Noon is 12 o'clock in the middle of the day.	3.82	0	4
A gem is a jewel or stone that is used in jewellery. A jewel is a precious stone used to decorate valuable things that you wear, such as rings or necklaces.	2.61	2.13	1.83

References

[Agirre and Soroa, 2009] Agirre, E. and Soroa, A. (2009). Personalizing pagerank for word sense disambiguation. In *Proceedings of the 12th Conference of the European Chapter of the Association for Computational Linguistics*, pages 33–41. Association for Computational Linguistics.

[Allen, 1987] Allen, J. (1987). Natural language understanding.

[BankPic, 2012] BankPic (2012). Financial institution picture. http://thetrustadvisor.com/wp-content/uploads/2012/08/Bank.jpg.

[ChoreographyPic, 2012] ChoreographyPic (2012). Choreography picture. http://4.bp.blogspot.com/-XNqetPxkQ2Q/UGkvKbFT-dI/AAAAAAAAGbk/ATEsIbv3cHk/s640/dance2.

[ClownPic, 2012] ClownPic (2012). Clown picture. http://www.featurepics.com/FI/Thumb300/20090530/Funny-Clown-Holding-Umbrella-1198395.jpg.

[Coster and Kauchak, 2011] Coster, W. and Kauchak, D. (2011). Simple english wikipedia: a new text simplification task. In *Proceedings of the 49th Annual Meeting of the Association for Computational Linguistics. Stroudsburg, PA: Association for Computational Linguistics*, pages 665–669.

[CottonPic, 2012] CottonPic (2012). Cotton picture. http://www.pastimesonline.ca/storage/blog-images/Cotton.jpg?__SQUARESPACE_CACHEVERSION=1291653372780.

[DancePic, 2012] DancePic (2012). Dance picture. http://americandanceguild.org/wp-content/uploads/2011/01/Rebecca-Rice-Dance-Lois-Greenfield-Web.jpg.

[DefencePic, 2012] DefencePic (2012). Plane banking picture. http://media.defenceindustrydaily.com/images/AIR_Super_Tucano_Seaside_Bank_lg.jpg.

[Hatzivassiloglou et al., 1999] Hatzivassiloglou, V., Klavans, J. L., and Eskin, E. (1999). Detecting text similarity over short passages: Exploring linguistic feature combinations via machine learning. In *Proceedings of the 1999 joint sigdat conference on empirical methods in natural language processing and very large corpora*, pages 203–212. Citeseer.

[Klein and Manning, 2003] Klein, D. and Manning, C. D. (2003). Accurate unlexicalized parsing. In *Proceedings of the 41st Annual Meeting on Association for Computational Linguistics-Volume 1*, pages 423–430. Association for Computational Linguistics.

[Landauer et al., 1997] Landauer, T. K., Laham, D., Rehder, B., and Schreiner, M. E. (1997). How well can passage meaning be derived without using word order? a comparison of latent semantic analysis and humans. In *Proceedings of the 19th annual meeting of the Cognitive Science Society*, pages 412–417.

[Li et al., Aug] Li, Y., Mclean, D., Bandar, Z., O'Shea, J., and Crockett, K. (Aug.). Sentence similarity based on semantic nets and corpus statistics. *Knowledge and Data Engineering, IEEE Transactions on*, 18(8):1138–1150.

[Li et al., 2006] Li, Y., McLean, D., Bandar, Z. A., O'shea, J. D., and Crockett, K. (2006). Sentence similarity based on semantic nets and corpus statistics. *Knowledge and Data Engineering, IEEE Transactions on*, 18(8):1138–1150.

[Manning et al., 2008] Manning, C. D., Raghavan, P., and Schütze, H. (2008). *Introduction to information retrieval*, volume 1. Cambridge University Press Cambridge.

[Matthiessen, 1986] Matthiessen, P. (1986). *Men's lives: the surfmen and baymen of the South Fork*. Random House.

[Mihalcea et al., 2006] Mihalcea, R., Corley, C., and Strapparava, C. (2006). Corpus-based and knowledge-based measures of text semantic similarity. In *Proceedings of the national conference on artificial intelligence*, volume 21, page 775. Menlo Park, CA; Cambridge, MA; London; AAAI Press; MIT Press; 1999.

[Miller, 1995] Miller, G. A. (1995). Wordnet: a lexical database for english. *Communications of the ACM*, 38(11):39–41.

[RiverPic, 2012] RiverPic (2012). Bank of a river. `http://1.bp.blogspot.com/_jGEuU1zFjq8/S7yLzJZuxfI/AAAAAAAACi8/h7chOGsf4kY/s1600/`.

[Rubenstein and Goodenough, 1965] Rubenstein, H. and Goodenough, J. B. (1965). Contextual correlates of synonymy. *Communications of the ACM*, 8(10):627–633.

[Rus et al., 2012] Rus, V., Mihai Lintean, C. M., William Baggett, N. N., and Morgan, B. (2012). The similar corpus: A resource to foster the qualitative understanding of semantic similarity of texts. Language Resource Evaluation Conference.

[Salton and Buckley, 1988] Salton, G. and Buckley, C. (1988). Term-weighting approaches in automatic text retrieval. *Information processing & management*, 24(5):513–523.

[SimpleWikipedia, 2012] SimpleWikipedia (2012). Simple english wikipedia. `http://simple.wikipedia.org/wiki/Main_Page`.

[Wikipedia, 2012] Wikipedia (2012). Wikipedia, the free dictionary. `http://en.wikipedia.org/wiki/Main_Page`.

[Wu and Salton, 1981] Wu, H. and Salton, G. (1981). A comparison of search term weighting: term relevance vs. inverse document frequency. In *ACM SIGIR Forum*, volume 16, pages 30–39. ACM.

www.ingramcontent.com/pod-product-compliance
Lightning Source LLC
LaVergne TN
LVHW042348060326
832902LV00006B/462